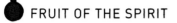 FRUIT OF THE SPIRIT

# GENTLENESS

**Fruit of the Spirit Study Guide Series**

Love

Joy

Peace

Patience

Kindness

Goodness

Faithfulness

Gentleness

Self-Control

CALVIN MILLER

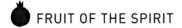 FRUIT OF THE SPIRIT

# GENTLENESS

Published in Nashville, Tennessee, by Thomas Nelson. Thomas Nelson is a trademark of Thomas Nelson, Inc.

Thomas Nelson, Inc., titles may be purchased in bulk for educational, business, fund-raising, or sales promotional use. For information, please e-mail SpecialMarkets@ThomasNelson.com.

Typesetting by Gregory C. Benoit Publishing, Old Mystic, CT

Unless otherwise noted, Scripture quotations are taken from the HOLY BIBLE: NEW INTERNATIONAL VERSION®. Copyright © 1973, 1978, 1984 by International Bible Society. Used by permission of Zondervan. All rights reserved.

Scripture quotations marked KJV are taken from King James Version of the Bible.

Scripture quotations marked TLB are taken from *The Living Bible*. © 1971. Used by permission of Tyndale House Publishers, Inc., Wheaton, Illinois 60189. All rights reserved.

ISBN: 978-1-4185-2843-0

*Printed in the United States of America*
08 09 10 11 12 RRD 9 8 7 6 5 4 3 2 1

# TABLE OF CONTENTS

But the fruit of the Spirit is love, joy, peace, patience, kindness, goodness, faithfulness, gentleness and self-control. Against such things there is no law.

—Galatians 5:22–23

# INTRODUCTION

Ego is the opponent of gentleness. When the ego takes over, gentleness disappears. There is a difference between gentleness and weakness. Gentleness is a characteristic of God that the Holy Spirit plants in his followers. Some people might argue that God's power and might negate his gentleness, but that's not true. God is simultaneously gentle and powerful.

In our world we see people asserting themselves and expecting everyone to conform to them. People develop celebrity self-images, believing that others will be awed just to be in their presence. These egotistical people are neither approachable nor gentle; they are a pain!

Gentleness, however, is God's way of dealing with his people. Gentleness allows us to approach God, climb up into his lap, and share our hearts. Gentleness allows God to visit with us where we are, because we can't go where he is. If anyone could ever demand respect and strike fear in everyone he meets, it is God. Yet God never acts this way; we do!

As God moves in and takes over our lives, we begin to see ourselves the way God sees us. We discover that few people are as impressed with us as we are. We realize that we live and breathe by the grace of God and nothing else.

God's presence in our lives comes forth in our gentleness in dealing with other people—the teenager working the fast-food drive-thru, the bank teller, the elderly couple shopping for groceries, and other drivers. When God's gentleness seeps out, we will be surprised at our responses. We become polite and considerate. We slow down and yield. We have less anxiety and take fewer pills for acid indigestion. God's gentleness has a way of curing many of our ills.

As we study together, let God's gentleness overtake your life and then watch as he transforms you into his image. Then, and only then, will you be able to accurately represent God to the world. Welcome to the journey.

# HOW TO USE THIS GUIDE

Galatians 5:22–23 is not a plan to achieve better faith. Rather, it is a description of God's personal gifts to all of us. If we follow God and seek his blessing, then the fruits of the Spirit are a natural overflow in our relationship with God. We are to grow in character so that one day we will reflect the image of our Lord.

This series of nine six-week studies will clearly focus your spiritual life to become more like Christ. Each study guide is divided into six weeks, and each of the six-week courses covers one of the fruits of the Spirit. Participants simply read each daily study and answer the questions at the end of each devotional. This prepares everyone for the group discussion at the end of the week.

Each week features a similar pattern that explores one aspect of that study's fruit of the Spirit. The first lesson establishes the aspect of the fruit to be explored throughout the week. The second lesson looks at the week's theme as it relates to God's purpose in the life of the believer. The third lesson looks at the week's theme as it relates to the believer's relationship with Christ. The fourth lesson explores how the fruit is relevant in service to others. And in the fifth lesson, the theme is related to personal worship. A sixth lesson is included as a bonus study, and focuses on either a biblical character who modeled this particular fruit, or a key parable that brings the theme into focus.

Each weeklong study should conclude in a group review. The weekly group discussion serves as a place to understand the practical side of the theme and receive encouragement and feedback on the journey to become more Christlike. For the study to have the character-transforming effect God desires, it is important for the participant to spend ten to twenty minutes a day reading the Scripture passage and the devotional, and to think through the two questions for the day. If each participant reads all of the questions beforehand, it greatly enhances the group dynamic. Each participant should choose three or four questions to discuss during the group session.

These simple guidelines will help make group time productive. Take a total of about forty-five minutes to answer and discuss the questions. Each person need not answer every question, but be sure all members participate. You can stimulate participation by having everyone respond to an icebreaker question. Have each group member answer the first of the six questions listed at the end of the week, and leave the remaining questions open-ended. Or, make up your own icebreaker question, such as: What color best represents the day you are having? What is your favorite movie? Or, how old were you when you had your first kiss?

No one should respond to all of the questions. Keep in mind that if you are always talking, the others are not. It is essential that everyone contribute. If you notice that someone is not participating, ask that group member which question is the most relevant. Be sensitive if something is keeping that member from contributing. Don't ask someone to read or pray aloud unless you know that the member is comfortable with such a task.

Always start and end your time with prayer. Sometimes it helps to have each person say what he or she plans to do with the lesson that week. Remember to reserve ten minutes for group prayer. You might want to keep a list of requests and answers to prayer at the back of this book.

# Week 1: Gentleness—The Approachable Life

*Memory Passage for the Week: Ruth 1:16*

### Day 1: Gentleness—The Approachable Life

Broken souls often become gentle because of all they have suffered, and, as a result, they can become the best counselors of God. Ruth 2:1–6, 22.

### Day 2: The Purpose of God in My Life

Hatred is uninviting, but gentleness makes others feel comfortable when we approach. Proverbs 10:12.

### Day 3: My Relationship with Christ

Children cause us to summon all the gentleness we can so we will not make them afraid. Childlikeness is the heart of gentility. Mark 10:13–16.

### Day 4: My Service to Others

God can also use people to minister who have been transformed by grace and have left their old, less-gentle natures behind—just as we all must do. Deuteronomy 28:53–57.

### Day 5: My Personal Worship

We should always remember the servant Messiah, the great king riding humbly on a donkey, and worship him in a spirit of gentleness. Zechariah 9:9.

### Day 6: A Character Study on Deborah

Judges 4:1–5:3

### Day 7: Group Discussion

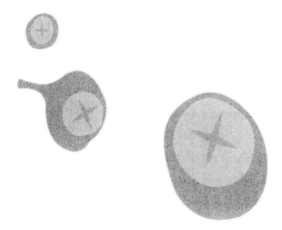

## Day 1: Gentleness—The Approachable Life
*Read Ruth 2:1–6, 22*

Ruth's mother-in-law encouraged her to go glean the fields of Boaz, Naomi's "kinsman-redeemer." In the first chapter of the book of Ruth, Naomi begged her friends to call her Mara, or "Miss Bitter," since life's circumstances made her an old and bitter person.

Cynicism and gentleness are opposite results of the same hardships. Some sufferings and trials break and wound people, but those who are broken and wounded become malleable—soft putty in God's hands. These broken souls know true gentleness because of all they have suffered—and they become God's best counselors.

But others react differently: they become cynical and hard. They are full of bitterness and brooding, unkind and harsh in their treatment of others. Naomi confessed to such bitterness.

But Naomi was home again in Bethlehem. Everything looks better when you're home. Her gentleness manifested in the advice she gave Ruth. But Boaz, too, was gentle in the advice he gave Ruth. "Don't go and glean in another field" (Ruth 2:8).

And Naomi encouraged Ruth to glean only in Boaz's fields, because "In someone else's field you might be harmed" (v. 22).

All in all Ruth might have been the apex of study on the spiritual fruits, particularly gentleness. Each aspect of the story sees gentleness creating an approachable life—the fine act of being so open and kind that all may approach us, and none will ever be afraid.

## Questions for Personal Reflection

1. Do you think your life is characterized by gentleness? Why or why not?

2. How does gentleness reflect the love of God? What are some situations in which you should be gentler?

## Day 2: The Purpose of God in My Life
*Read Proverbs 10:12*

Hate does indeed stir dissension—but gentleness stirs camaraderie and openness into our lives. Filled with gentleness, we are able to live out the purposes of God in our lives. Gentleness causes people to see us as approachable. Only then will they cease being afraid of us. Only then can we truly minister to them.

Ministry *is* the purpose of God in our lives. Therefore it is mandatory that we embrace gentleness in order to fulfill this purpose. The writer of Proverbs said that to harbor hate or permit ourselves any grudge keeps us in such dissension that a gentle spirit becomes impossible.

"Hatred stirs ... Love covers" (Proverbs 10:12) really means:

> **Hate** agitates ... **love** pacifies.
> **Hate** boils in the soul ... **love** sails on a placid sea of forgiveness.
> **Hate** spreads its cancerous tentacles ... **love** removes the ugly scar tissue of resentment and replaces it with the clean, healed tissue of health.

Watch a man who is filled with grudges. He will vent, spew, and be unable to talk without a spirit of malevolence owning his speech.

Watch a woman under the compulsion of love. She will serve Christ and saturate her service with gentleness.

## Questions for Personal Reflection

1. Are you approachable? If not, what keeps others at a distance? If so, what is it

that makes people comfortable around you?

2. What is the connection between love and gentleness? Why is it impossible to

love someone and not be gentle?

## Day 3: My Relationship with Christ
*Read Mark 10:13–16*

Children are great students of human nature. Their innocence endows them with an ability to correctly measure things. While their innocence might cause them to sometimes trust those they shouldn't, such as abusers, children tend to easily build rapport with truly gentle people.

In today's passage the disciples rebuked parents who brought their children to be blessed. No doubt the disciples were trying to protect Jesus. After all, he was busy. Mothers are incredibly hard-working, busy people as well. But many people get so caught up in efficiency that they leave true ministry in the dust. So instead of joining the men in the crowd, who castigated the mothers and their children, Jesus sided with the women.

To children, grandparents seem studied and kind. They have enough gray hair and wrinkles from enduring the pain of life that their eyes are mellow with understanding. No wonder children love them. And grandparents are rarely in a hurry. With so many years under their belts, often they have learned the futility of hurry and have the wisdom to slow down a bit to savor the important things in life, like family.

Kind eyes and an unhurried agenda make all of us more approachable, and they leave children unafraid. Jesus was not a grandparent, but I like to think he had kind eyes and was so unhurried children that were never afraid of him.

They came to him. He blessed them. And the Son of God, who bore the intense burden of redeeming the planet, was able to be interrupted by those who needed his blessing. Being easily interruptible is a virtue of gentleness.

"Let the little children come," Jesus said, "for the kingdom of God belongs to such as these" (Mark 10:14). Heaven is a place where trust and gentleness are abundant. Live your life in such a way as to reflect heaven's virtues, and you will be quite at home when you arrive there.

## Questions for Personal Reflection

1. What is your response when someone interrupts you? Are you kind and gentle or are you rude and disrespectful?

2. If your gentleness is an indication of your love for God, how much might an acquaintance say you love God?

## Day 4: My Service to Others

*Read Deuteronomy* 28:53–57

This passage in Deuteronomy is a grisly consideration. Cannibalism, said Moses, would be the lot of Israel under siege. They would greedily devour their own children as evidence that the last shred of human compassion was gone.

Even so, the words "gentle" and "sensitive" are used four times in this passage. The concept of gentleness is a striking contrast to the cannibalism mentioned in the same breath.

All of this begs the question, What is the difference between all things fierce and all things kind? For every Christian, the answer is the word *gentle*. "Gentleness" is what happens to fierceness when Jesus touches it with grace.

I have never gotten over the transforming effect of salvation on human life. Mean and abrasive people suddenly give up their savage behavior and become approachable. That is why we minister to others. Ministry-centered people are not always people who are naturally gentle. Often they are people who have been remodeled by grace and have left their old natures far behind.

Probably those who heard Moses' discourse doubted whether good, believing Israelites could ever become cannibals. Moses' point was that, without the grace of God, we would be worse off than we can possibly imagine.

## Questions for Personal Reflection

1. How have you been the beneficiary of someone else's gentleness?

2. How has his love transformed your attitude toward others?

# Day 5: My Personal Worship
*Read Zechariah 9:9*

Jesus rode into Jerusalem on a colt, the foal of a donkey. The mood upon his arrival was wild celebration—the Messiah had come! We cannot really imagine how Palm Sunday would have been affected if Jesus rode in on a great white steed. Would the celebration have been as wonderful? All that can be said is that our worship transcends glory when God—or in this case Jesus—is approachable. We offer our freest praise when we are unafraid.

Is not God holy? Are we not to live in sobriety and the fear of God? Surely the fear of God is *the beginning of wisdom* (Psalm 111:10). But the whole point of God becoming a human is to take the austerity out of our relationship with Christ. Christ called the austere God "Daddy," or "Abba, Father."

In Christ, God's gentleness was made known. Christ came to us on a donkey—he conquered death and hell and left no question about his greatness, but his conquest inspired the utmost of human worship on Palm Sunday. As the Gospel writers recalled, the people shouted two things: "Hosanna!" a Messianic cheer, and "Blessed is He who comes in the name of the Lord!" a Messianic salutation (Mark 11:9). This paints a picture of two kinds of Messianic Israel. One is the Davidic (The White Horse King) Messiah. The other is the Isaianic (The Donkey-Riding Gentle Servant) Messiah. Jesus consciously opted to display the servant-

Messiah image. His gentle entrance to his final week of life leaves no doubt of that.

The God who created the cosmos and ordered the tides is ours in Christ, and we cry in utter praise, "Hosanna!" Blessed is the gentle one who comes in the name of the Lord.

Our wildest praise is born in the wake of his kind love.

## Questions for Personal Reflection

1. What are the situations that cause you to offer praise to God?

2. What are those things that interfere with your ability to praise God?

# Day 6: Deborah—Charisma in True Leadership

*Read Judges 4:1—5:3*

Deborah was a popular judge in Israel. Her countrymen went to her to settle disputes. Deborah led with gentle leadership, and she judged the nation of Israel with a heart after God. She wasn't exactly a Joan of Arc–type of warrior, but she did receive word from the Lord that Israel was to go to war. So she acted as God's emissary to summon the nation to battle. She sent for Barak, a warrior leader who was insecure about his ability to challenge Sisera, a formidable opponent (Judges 4:1–3).

Yet Deborah's leadership, even in war, was fraught with gentleness. Gentle leadership always makes a leader approachable, securing closeness between the leader and those he or she leads.

Deborah sent Barak this message: "The LORD, the God of Israel, commands you: 'Go, take with you ten thousand men of Naphtali and Zebulun and lead the way to Mount Tabor. I will lure Sisera, the commander of Jabin's army, with his chariots and his troops to the Kishon River and give him into your hands'" (vv. 6–7).

But Barak was insecure: "If you go with me, I will go" (v. 8).

Who knows exactly what he meant? Perhaps he was saying, "I need a little moral support," or, "Israel will respond better if the chief judge of the land is in the leadership circle for this military campaign." But Deborah sensed his fear and offered him this censure: "I will go with you. But because of the way you are going about this, the honor will not be yours, for the LORD will hand Sisera over to a woman" (v. 9).

After the rout of Sisera, it was the lowly Jael, the wife of Heber the Kenite, who invited the fleeing Sisera in for a nap and drove a tent stake through his head while he slept (v. 21). It was Jael, not Barak, who received all the credit for dispatching the evil *generalissimo*.

Deborah and Barak sang a song of high praise after the battle, once more affirming that gentle leadership furnishes both the stamina and joy for every crisis.

> *When the princes in Israel take the lead,*
> > *when the people willingly offer themselves—*
> > *praise the LORD!*
> *Hear this, you kings! Listen, you rulers!*
> > *I will sing to the LORD, I will sing;*
> > *I will make music to the LORD, the God of Israel."*
> —Judges 5:2–3

Gentleness is a singer.

It prefers soft lullabies.

It indulges in ballads that celebrate the lives of those who thought themselves fearful till they heard the gentle song.

Gentleness always sings.

## Questions for Personal Reflection

1. What song does your life sing? Is it a song of gentleness? If not, what needs

to happen in order for your life to be filled with God's gentleness?

2. How has the absence of gentleness damaged your relationships? How might

things have been different if gentleness had been evident?

# Day 7: Group Discussion

The following questions should take about forty-five minutes to answer and discuss. Each member should answer the first question, leaving the remaining questions open-ended. Everyone need not answer, but be sure all members participate.

1.  *How does gentleness make someone approachable? Why is this important?*

2.  *How can your gentleness help you reach people who don't know God?*

3.  *Why is it so hard to be humble in today's world? What is the relationship between humility and gentleness?*

4.  *How would you behave if God had not imparted his goodness into your life?*

5.   What is the role of gentleness in regard to our offering of praise to God?

6.   What are some ministries that need to be filled with people who demonstrate gentleness? Why is gentleness so important in these ministries?

## Week 2: Gentleness—Winning Others to Christ

*Memory Passage for the Week: Philippians 4:5*

### Day 1: Gentleness—Winning Others to Christ

Gentleness always wins but never gloats over its victories. Acts 9:36–40.

### Day 2: The Purpose of God in My Life

In a day of loud services and loud disciples, the idea that God whispers gently is certainly welcome. 1 Kings 19:11–14.

### Day 3: My Relationship with Christ

Gentleness is the great cosmetic that adorns the human spirit. An unfading and gentle spirit is a valuable beauty that comes in neither creams nor lotions. 1 Peter 3:1–6.

### Day 4: My Service to Others

We look to the example of gentle Gaius, in the book of 3 John, and follow his gentle ways as the kingdom of God expands. 3 John 5–8.

### Day 5: My Personal Worship

Ruth and Naomi's gentleness did not win them a moment of grand worship in a splendid tabernacle, but it did teach them that life itself can become a worship experience. Ruth 1:16–17.

### Day 6: A Character Study on Phoebe, Priscilla, & Mary

Romans 16:1–6

### Day 7: Group Discussion

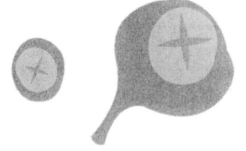

# Day 1: Gentleness—Winning Others to Christ
*Read Acts 9:36–40*

According to the book of Acts, Dorcas was a gentle woman who was always doing good and helping the poor. She fell ill and died, but after she was dead, all the articles of clothing and needlework she had done were brought to her deathbed to celebrate her creativity.

When gentle people pass on, they leave a terrible hole in life. When the power-hungry pass on, people react quite differently. When the miserly and stingy leave, there are very few people who miss them. Do you remember when the Ghost of Christmas Yet to Come showed old Scrooge his coming funeral? Nobody wanted to go. The life of Dorcas, on the other hand, was a testament to her gentility. Many crowded around to mourn her death but also to honor her gentle life. They celebrated the gentle, outgoing, and creative spirit that she used to bless others. Gentleness was Christ's gift to Dorcas, and Dorcas generously gave that gift to the world.

Gentleness is a great evangelist. It is the best witness of the gentle living and the best witness of the gentle dead. Gentleness wins. It is important for every Christian to ask him or herself, "Have I developed an outgoing gentleness that seeks to use my talents to cause the world to celebrate Jesus?"

In the end, Dorcas was miraculously raised from the dead and went on to live for a few more years. One can't help but wonder what happened when she died the second time—perhaps another party? Another celebration of her gentle life by her gentle converts? I like to think so, for gentleness always wins and never gloats over its victories.

## Questions for Personal Reflection

1. Will you be remembered as a person who gave his or her life in gentle service to others? Why or why not?

2. What might you be able to do to portray God to a doubting world?

# Day 2: The Purpose of God in My Life
*Read 1 Kings 19:11–14*

In the fiery life of Elijah, God spoke in a gentle whisper. This Sinai whisper asked Elijah, "What are you doing here?" Elijah was frightened by Jezebel, who threatened to put him to death. Elijah, who had recently called down fire from heaven on Mt. Carmel, had run for his life into the pits of personal depression.

Perhaps under the juniper tree in 1 Kings 19, he became so depressed he forgot who he was, whom he worked for, and what God's purpose for his life really was. Then came the whispering God. God wants no one to live ill-informed about his purpose in life, so he speaks to us.

First came a wind so great and powerful that the rocks were shattered (v. 11), but the Lord was not in the wind.

Then came an earthquake, but the Lord was not in the earthquake (v. 11).

Next, a fire roared, but God was not in the fire (v. 12).

And after the fire, a gentle whisper, no doubt the kind of quiet that strained the ears (v. 13). Suddenly, the Lord was there.

God's whisper defines both our calling and our own gentle manner of living it out. We must listen for him.

## Questions for Personal Reflection

1. Why do we miss God's whispers? How does our affection for the spectacular

affect our ability to hear him when he quietly calls?

2. Maybe you have looked for God in places where he wasn't. How have those

experiences affected your ability to hear God now?

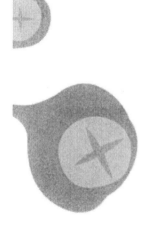

# Day 3: My Relationship with Christ
*Read 1 Peter 3:1–6*

The gospel of Christ has immensely liberated women, and how grateful all of us are to Jesus for the liberation. But it was not always so. In the first century, women were often at the mercy of their husbands in every aspect of things social or political. Many women came to Christ and then longed for their husbands to be saved. This could best be accomplished, said Peter, if these women lived lives of submission and demonstrated to the world the sheer power of gentleness.

Words were not the strongest way for these women to evangelize. How does a gentle spirit witness?

- Their inner lives showed "purity" and "reverence" (1 Peter 3:2).
- Their quiet spirits had an "unfading beauty" (v. 4).
- They "[made] themselves beautiful" by their gentility and modesty (v. 5).

We should not assume that Peter was saying that women should never wear makeup in order to be beautiful. Cosmetics are one of many things people use to enhance God's natural gifts, but loveliness is essentially an inward matter. It cannot be created by mere cosmetics. By showing the glow of inner beauty and a spirit of humility and gentleness, one's relationship with Christ shines through beautifully for all to see.

## Questions for Personal Reflection

1. How might your nonverbal actions help win someone to Christ?

2. How might your nonverbal actions prevent someone from coming to know

Christ?

# Day 4: My Service to Others
*Read 3 John 5–10*

"It was for the sake of the Name that they went out, receiving no help from the pagans," said John. "We ought therefore to show hospitality to such men that we may work together for the truth" (3 John 7–8). This letter was gentle, from a gentle pen, addressed to the gentle Gaius. Yet its gentleness throbbed with purpose. These people were not in charge of their world—legally, Caesar was—but they seriously desired to win their world with a witness to the truth.

The letter is short, with barely enough verses to contrast the gentility of Gaius with the arch-devilry of Diotrephes. Still, consider the contrast:

**Gaius:** He continued to walk in the truth (v. 3) and lead others to walk in the truth (v. 4). He was gentle to strangers (v. 5), he showed hospitality to all (v. 8), and he taught others to defend the Name (v. 7). Gaius was the very picture of a winning gentleness that served others and drew them to Christ.

**Diotrephes** (vv. 9–10): He was ambitious and craved power. He was a malicious gossip. He was inhospitable, even to good people, and was hasty to throw people out of the church.

John advised Gaius and others to imitate the gentle life and to continue ministering in gentle ways as the kingdom of God expanded. What good advice for the current church! Let us bypass the those who hunger after abusive power, and let us live the gentle life that wins.

## Questions for Personal Reflection

1. Are you more like Gaius or Diotrephes? Why?

2. What are three things you could do to become more like Gaius?

# Day 5: My Personal Worship
*Read Ruth 1:16–17*

To think of gentleness is to think of the book of Ruth. This book is a beautiful little stopover of grace sandwiched between sagas of the judges and histories of kings and national prophets. Ruth isn't just a book you study; it's like a new pair of shoes you put on, only to find your heels winged with the noblest part of the human spirit.

"Intreat me not to leave thee," Ruth said to Naomi (Ruth 1:16 KJV). These wounded women spoke in prose as elegant as Shakespeare. But their elegance was steeped in tenderness—and gentleness. They became gentle as widows, alone and unsupported in a society that did not always take care of its women.

Ruth traveled along when Naomi went home, bereaved and penniless. Did their gentleness win a moment of grand worship in a splendid tabernacle? No, but it taught them that life itself can become a worship experience. God is a balm for the pain of the gentle. So Ruth turned to her mother-in-law and said, "Where you go I will go, and where you stay I will stay. Your people will be my people and your God my God. Where you die I will die, and there I will be buried. May the LORD deal with me, be it ever so severely, if anything but death separates you and me" (vv. 16–17).

How blessed are all those who make gentle but steely commitments. This is the spine of the tender book of Ruth.

## Questions for Personal Reflection

1. How does your life compare to the life of Ruth? Are you as gentle as she was?

2. How can God use a gentle spirit to change generations to come? Do you

believe he can use you for that purpose? Why or why not?

## Day 6: Phoebe, Priscilla, & Mary—The Gentle Women Ministers
*Read Romans 16:1–6*

Many names appear in a list of outstanding gentle saints, but leading the list are three very noble women: Phoebe, Priscilla, and Mary. Phoebe was the courageous servant who volunteered to carry Paul's letter across hundreds of miles of open road to see that it got safely to the congregation meeting in Rome. Priscilla had the gift of hospitality to the point that she opened her home to house the newly formed churches that surrounded Paul's missionary enterprises. And Mary, simply put, worked hard!

These women were leaders in the early Christian church, but theirs was not just an issue of courageous leadership. There is hidden in the sixteenth chapter of Paul's letter to the church in Rome a commendation of gentle courage. These women were unafraid of the challenges the kingdom of God had laid upon them. And while they were undoubtedly like many women of their day, who were well acquainted with and adept in domestic duties, it was not for these kinds of duties that Paul cited the quality of their leadership.

Phoebe, Priscilla, and Mary were given commissions to carry out tasks for the sake of the kingdom. But even the importance of what God had called them to do pales beside the manner in which they did it. There is something so gentle in the brief passage in Romans 16 that tells us these women were not just thorough in what God asked them to do; they were *gentle* in the manner in which they did it.

Is this reading too much into the character of these saints? After all, we don't know them personally. Is it possible they were grumpy or gossipy or critical in nature? I think not. One cannot help but feel the warmth of their gentility that oozes from Paul's commendation. It is clear these were women of strong resolve, but they were not demanding souls who forced others to recognize their leadership. They were role models for Christian womanhood, not feminism.

We have every obligation to be ministers of Christ, but we are to make none afraid of our ministry. Our gentleness should be like that of Phoebe, Priscilla, and Mary: with a warm and inviting spirit, taking care of the business of God, and loving every needy person in our path.

"Rejoice in the Lord, always. I will say it again: Rejoice! Let your gentleness be evident to all. The Lord is near," Paul reminded the Philippians (Philippians 4:4–5). The Lord will one day break into history in his wonderful second coming. When he comes, he should find us winning the world in such a gentle way that we make no one afraid.

## Questions for Personal Reflection

1. When you think of the word "gentleness," what kind of actions come to

mind?

2. How many of those actions do you practice often? Which of those actions

would you like to practice more often?

# Day 7: Group Discussion

The following questions should take about forty-five minutes to answer and discuss. Each member should answer the first question, leaving the remaining questions open-ended. Everyone need not answer, but be sure all members participate.

1.  *Share about a time when you have seen someone be firm and take a strong stand while still remaining gentle.*

2.  *Why does it often go against our initial instincts to be gentle?*

3.   *How can our lives be strengthened through gentleness?*

4.   *How can we use gentleness to strengthen the lives of people around us?*

5. If you lived in Old Testament times, would you have been a candidate for being in the lineage of Christ? Why or why not?

6. How can the comparison between Gaius and Diotrephes help someone understand the value of gentleness?

# Week 3: Gentleness—Ego Displacement

*Memory Passage for the Week: Ephesians 4:2*

### Day 1: Gentleness—Ego Displacement

We need to displace our egos with gentleness, abandon power, and greet others in the house of God with a non-abusive spirit. 2 Samuel 18:1–5.

### Day 2: The Purpose of God in My Life

God has a way of teaching humility to those whose towering egos have never desired to learn the art. Isaiah 8:6–8.

### Day 3: My Relationship with Christ

There is little question that those who achieve gentleness have learned to use in order to discipline the thoughts of their hearts. 2 Corinthians 10:1–6.

### Day 4: My Service to Others

When anyone is erroneously proclaiming something as the truth, it requires a gentle approach to straighten it out. Acts 18:24–26; 19:1–5.

### Day 5: My Personal Worship

Gentleness rarely appeals to people of power, but it learns worship in the simple acts of openness and integrity. Luke 18:10–13.

### Day 6: A Character Study on John Mark

Acts 12:25; 13:4–5, 13; 15:36–39; Colossians 4:10; 2 Timothy 4:11; Philemon 24; 1 Peter 5:13

### Day 7: Group Discussion

# Day 1: Gentleness—Ego Displacement
*Read 2 Samuel 18:1–5*

David felt the visitation of old sins. His affair with Bathsheba demonstrated that he was capable of using power to get what he wanted in life. But when he saw the same tendency in the life of his son, Absalom, he must have been cut to the heart. For Absalom, like his father before him, resorted to power to get what he wanted in life.

Power. What is this swaggering force that makes us puff ourselves up with grandiose self-images? What is there in power that drives us to use abusive politics and cruel force to get what we want regardless of the cost to others? The world has been a vast weeping planet for centuries because of the lust for power.

Power isn't the problem of only swaggering warlords like Absalom. Power causes people in corporations to squelch their competition and hurt employees in lower positions. Power causes ordinarily decent men and women to "do unto others *before* others do unto them." Power sponsors a new definition of the Golden Rule: "He who has the gold, rules." Nowadays the rich and powerful can buy the moon—but the souls of the poor find justice unavailable to them because they do not have the cash.

But nowhere is power abuse uglier than when people use ungodly power to arrive at plateaus of control that keep the body of Christ caught up in competition and greed. We need to displace our egos with gentleness, abandon power, and greet others in the kingdom of God with a non-abusive spirit.

## Questions for Personal Reflection

1. Do you ever feel your desire for power getting out of control? Explain.

2. How can your commitment to God keep your power in check?

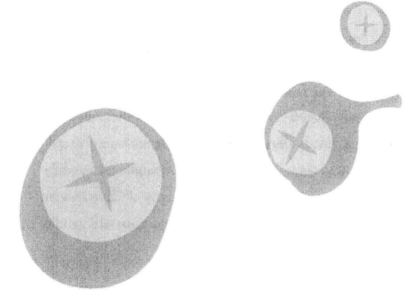

# Day 2: The Purpose of God in My Life
*Read 2 Samuel 18:1–5*

It is easy to deal harshly with others but suddenly plead for gentleness when they deal with us. But when we plead for gentleness on behalf of those who don't deserve it, we approach a state of *grace*. David was king, but he was a somewhat whipped soul in this passage. Life was hard. God had given David a great empire. But when David yielded to sin, the results of that sin tore into his home life with ferocity: the incest of Amnon and Tamar, two of his children, and the revolt of Absalom, his crown prince.

One can only imagine what went through David's mind as he looked out over columns of his own soldiers, ready to crush Absalom's mutinous army because it threatened the king's life. The king must have had tears in his eyes as he watched this horrible civil war unfold. Yet he told Joab and the other generals, "Deal gently with the young man Absalom for my sake" (2 Samuel 18:5).

Gentleness is the virtue of fathers and mothers who have cried over their children. You would think disobedient children would cause their parents to act with severity. Instead it causes their parents to weep over the huge fractures in the family. David was a weeping father, and his gentleness came bathed in the gift of his tears.

Gentleness in the face of insurrection is a godly response. What happened in the heart of the king to sponsor such an attitude? Life. He was older and wiser and learned at last that life knows only one great requirement: obedience to God. This obedience inspired him to treat his child with gentleness.

Is this not God's lesson for us as well? When we treat others with a gentle spirit, we have indeed seen our calling to Christian service. For being like God is always to give others more than they deserve.

## Questions for Personal Reflection

1. How might your gentle treatment of someone affect your ability to have a long-term relationship?

2. What must you do to develop gentleness in your life?

# Day 3: My Relationship with Christ
*Read 2 Corinthians 10:1–6*

The art of ego displacement is only fine when we displace our egos with Jesus Christ. In this passage Paul suggested how this can be done. We are all fighting a spiritual war in hopes to transform ourselves and the world, and the battlefield is our minds. But the battle can only be won if we understand that we are not fighting with ordinary military weapons; we are fighting with our minds. We are not fighting *hard;* we are fighting *smart!*

We are called to make Christ the Lord of our gray matter. When we let Christ's mind dwell in us, our minds achieve a new dynamic. This dynamic enables us to be the most creative and achieving people that we can be.

Christianity has always been involved in warfare of the mind. It is here that God gives us the power to outthink and outpray the sinister forces of Satan, the prince of this world. So our intentions are our broadswords. Our dreams of the kingdom are our tanks and rifles. Our commitment is our ammunition. And our minds are the bunkers where we deploy God's powerful and unbeatable winning strategy.

But how does all this warlike verbiage build ego displacement?

We will show the world that arrogant armaments cannot stand before the innocent power of gentleness. We arrive at this gentleness by taking every thought captive and making it obedient to Christ. This means that between the time a thought enters our minds and the time we let it out of our mouths, we have made it something that Jesus would say. Will such a battle tactic work? Can such disciplined gentleness win? Let us wait for his appearing, and we shall see that the answer is yes.

## Questions for Personal Reflection

1. What has more control of your life—your ego or God's gentleness?

2. Who is winning the battle for your mind—God or Satan? What ammunition is being used on each side?

# Day 4: My Service to Others
*Read Acts 18:24–26; 19:1–5*

Acts 19:1–5 shows how much harm good preachers of bad doctrine can really do. Without a doubt, Apollos was a great communicator. Acts 18:25 says that he preached the Word of God with great fervor. It was impossible to fall asleep during his sermons! But because he preached heresy, it would have been better if those who heard him had fallen asleep. False doctrine in the hands of great communicators represents a kind of double threat.

But this must be said for Apollos: he was open to the truth, and when Priscilla and Aquila took him home for a few lessons in Bible doctrine, his teaching improved. Apollos was to be commended for learning, and Priscilla and Aquila were to be commended for straightening him out.

A popular cable evangelist once taught that the Trinity should be expanded to a *septinity*—a sevenfold godhead rather than a threefold godhead. This concept of the godhead was to be made larger by including the seven spirits that ministered before the throne in John's apocalypse (Revelation 4:5). Some faithful, more theological souls were able to take him aside and teach him how to expound the word more positively—and to keep sound doctrine. As in the case of Apollos, the errant evangelist corrected his doctrine and was properly commended.

False teachers can sometimes be reclaimed, and the best way to approach these situations is with a gentle spirit. That means displacing our own egos with a serving spirit in order to keep the church's teaching pure.

## Questions for Personal Reflection

1. How do you know when you are being taught false doctrine?

2. What should you do when you are being taught falsely?

# Day 5: My Personal Worship
*Read Luke 18:10–13*

Long ago I wrote a poem called "The Pharisee." In its words I hope that
you will see why ego is so hard to displace:

> *Do you see him there? The public square*
> *Is just the place to photograph his face*
> *Etched with earnest lines. He weeps. He cares.*
> *He thunders recompense, intones his grace.*
> *We must unfold our hands and then applaud.*
> *And gape at academic piety.*
> *Degrees and robes can make us look like God,*
> *Festoon us in neon humility.*
>
> *ENCORE! ENCORE! Pray earnestly, God-friend.*
> *The quadraphonic tone of your Amen*
> *Will send the curtain flying up again.*
> *The seats are packed with rapt humanity.*
>
> *Kneel closer to the lights so we may see.*
> *Dear God, is this unticketed and free?*[1]

A Pharisee is one whose religion is mostly performance. Publicans, on the other hand, find their needs too great to try to keep up with that level of acting with God.

Remember, Jesus called the Pharisees hypocrites, and *hypocrite* means "actor's mask." Gentleness is naked-faced. It never strives to be pretty, only honest. So the publican goes down to his house justified because integrity has replaced egotism. Gentleness rarely appeals to people of power, but it learns worship in the simple acts of openness and integrity.

## Questions for Personal Reflection

1. How can you keep from becoming like the Pharisees?

2. How does integrity relate to gentleness? Can you have one without the other?

# Day 6: John Mark—The Gentleness of a Missionary Witness

*Read Acts 12:25; 13:4–5, 13; 15:36–39; Colossians 4:10; 2 Timothy 4:11; Philemon 24; 1 Peter 5:13*

Any thorough discussion of John Mark must stem from somewhat random selections from the New Testament. It is implied that the young man who fled from Gethsemane naked was John Mark, and that the Last Supper was held in his home earlier that same evening (Mark 14:51). By examining eight different passages, we can piece together a biography of sorts:

1. **Acts 12:25.** After Paul's trip to Jerusalem at the beginning of the missionary enterprise out of Antioch, Paul and Barnabas took John Mark with them to the city of Antioch. Paul's missionary journeys originated there.

2. **Acts 13:4–5.** When Paul and Barnabas began their first missionary journey, John Mark was their traveling companion and helper.

3. **Acts 13:13.** John Mark left the missionaries in Perga of Pamphilia for unknown reasons. But it seems that the apostle Paul considered him a quitter.

4. **Acts 15:36–39.** In preparation for the second missionary journey, Paul and Barnabas had a fierce quarrel over John Mark. Barnabas wanted to take him on the second missionary

journey, but Paul did not. So John Mark and Barnabas formed their own missionary team and went to Cyprus to evangelize, while Paul picked Silas and returned to Asia Minor.

5. **Colossians 4:10.** This verse teaches that Barnabas and John Mark were cousins. This makes sense, since the church in Jerusalem met at John Mark's house and Barnabas was connected with that church (Acts 4:36).

6. **2 Timothy 4:11.** By this time Paul confessed he wanted to see John Mark, who was very helpful to him in his ministry.

7. **Philemon 24.** Here Paul had a friendly attitude toward John Mark, suggesting they came to some kind of reconciliation.

8. **1 Peter 5:13.** This reference connected John Mark and Peter. Many scholars believe that John Mark's Gospel really comes from Peter's eyewitness accounts of the life of Christ.

In all, John Mark was a key figure of the New Testament who, despite his forceful nature, allowed his gentle spirit to witness the gentle Christ in a way history will not forget.

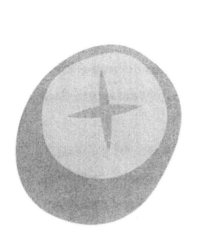

## Questions for Personal Reflection

1. Based on your personal qualities, would Paul have wanted you as a companion on his missionary journeys? Why or why not?

2. What can you do to become a person of noble character?

# Day 7: Group Discussion

The following questions should take about forty-five minutes to answer and discuss. Each member should answer the first question, leaving the remaining questions open-ended. Everyone need not answer, but be sure all members participate.

1.   *What are the things in our world that stand in the way of our being gentle?*

2.   *How can we overcome some of the things mentioned in question 1?*

3. *In what areas of life do we most need to bring our thoughts into the captivity of Christ?*

4. *How can God use a gentle spirit to help correct doctrinal errors?*

5.  *How are we affected by modern-day Pharisees?*

6.  *Would a summary of your life reveal a character of gentleness? Why or why not?*

# Week 4: Gentleness—Childlike Godliness

*Memory Passage for the Week: Luke 10:21*

### Day 1: Gentleness—Childlike Godliness

God often speaks gently to us, as we might speak to a child. We need to listen carefully to hear him. 1 Samuel 3:1–10.

### Day 2: The Purpose of God in My Life

God's tenderness toward his children models the sort of gentleness he would love to see in them. Isaiah 49:15.

### Day 3: My Relationship with Christ

It is amazing how the full surrender of the most trivial things enlivens our relationship not only with Christ but with the whole world. John 6:8–9.

### Day 4: My Service to Others

God is gentle. His childlike gentleness is exactly what we need as we consider ministering to others. James 3:13–18.

### Day 5: My Personal Worship

The great thing about Christian truth is its simplicity. Children can celebrate its gentle doctrines as readily as those who are older and sometimes more grudging. Matthew 21:14–17.

### Day 6: A Character Study on Barnabas

Acts 4:36–37; 11:19–24

### Day 7: Group Discussion

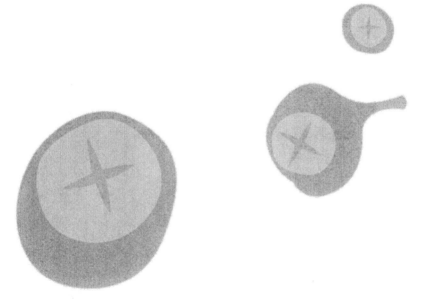

## Day 1: Gentleness—Childlike Godliness
*Read 1 Samuel 3:1–10*

The old prophet Eli instructed little Samuel (after hearing his name called for the third time), telling Samuel that if he heard his name called again, it might be God, so he should say, 'Speak, Lord, for your servant hears you!'"

Consider the tenderness in this gentle metaphor. The God who thundered on Sinai called Samuel so quietly, at first he didn't realize it was God at all.

God speaks to us gently so that he won't frighten us. He comes so softly that he whispered to Elijah and answered Gideon with no words—only fleece. He went to Moses in a burning bush and spoke to Paul in such a way that his traveling companions could not make out his words.

"Speak, Lord, for your servant is listening," said the boy Samuel, and God's gentleness initiated in Samuel an enduring, vital lesson in obedience and blessing. God made a gentle entrance, but Samuel's calling made a dynamic impact on Israel. Samuel helped the nation from the era of the judges to the era of the monarchy. He anointed the first two kings of Israel—one of them became Israel's greatest king. He blessed battles and condemned sin.

When Samuel began his role as national prophet, Israel was a loose confederacy of clans and tribes; but at the end of his life, Israel was a nation on the way to walled cities, levied armies, and world-class status.

Yet all the while, God spoke gently to the prophet, and used David, the second king he anointed, to sing his gentle praises to a nation.

## Questions for Personal Reflection

1. When was the last time God spoke gently to you? What did he say?

2. What are some areas of life about which you want God to speak to you?

## Day 2: The Purpose of God in My Life
*Read Isaiah 49:15*

Gentleness is the tenderness God uses to relate to us. The prophet Isaiah's metaphor asks: Can a nursing mother forget her child? Never! But even if she could, God will never forget his children. God is tender—he is gentle with all of us. It is his purpose to meet the heinous crimes of tyrants with gentility. The world is a brutal and ugly place, but in the midst of this horror, God gently reminds us of his purpose.

Between the years 1534 and 1584, a pageant was performed on the steps of the Coventry Cathedral. A lullaby was written and sung in the pageant every year. This haunting theme by an unknown author clung to the souls of those who heard it; it was a lullaby Bethlehem mothers sang to their little ones who were massacred in their cribs by the wicked Herod.

*Lul-lay, Thou little tiny Child,*
*Bye-bye, lul-loo, lul-lay.*
*Lul-lay, Thou little tiny Child,*
*Bye-bye, lul-loo, lul-lay.*

*O sisters, too, how may we do*
*For to preserve this day?*
*This poor Youngling for whom we sing,*
*Bye-bye, lul-loo, lul-lay.*

*Herod the king in his raging*
*Charged he hath this day*
*His men of might, in his own sight,*
*All children young to slay.*

*Then woe is me, poor Child for Thee,*
*And ever morn and day,*
*For thy parting nor say or sing,*
*Bye-bye, lul-loo, lul-lay.*[2]

Oh, the gentle tenderness of a caring God! God never forgets his children. Gently he loves us. Gently he leads us to celebrate his purpose in our lives.

## Questions for Personal Reflection

1. How could we develop gentleness that is as consistent as God's?

2. Based on the way you care for others, do you have evidence of God's gentleness in your life?

# Day 3: My Relationship with Christ
*Read John 6:8–9*

The greatest catering feat of all time was pulled off by one Savior, one servant, and one child. The child said, "Here's my lunch." The servant said, "Here's his lunch, but it cannot possibly feed this many!" The Savior said, "Make the crowd sit down."

The world was about to be amazed at how far a boy's lunch could go. We are likewise amazed that those things we surrender to Jesus—though they seem little—may be used of God in ways too impressive for us to imagine.

Childlike gentleness appealed to the servant. The servant's obedience appealed to the Savior, and eating appealed to everyone.

There is a story, long celebrated among Christians, of this boy who supplied the meal. The boy was very proud as the Master took his lunch and began to divide it among the masses. As the boy watched Jesus breaking his loaves, he must have said, "That's my bread!" When Jesus passed his fish out to the crowd, he must have thought, "That's my fish." But as Jesus kept breaking and feeding the crowd of thousands, the little boy must have realized, "That's not my bread and fish anymore."

Gentleness takes the smallest assets and multiplies them so they serve in wider ways than we can imagine. It is amazing how the full surrender of the most trivial things enlivens our relationship not only with Christ but with the whole world.

## Questions for Personal Reflection

1. What small thing can you give to God? What do you expect him to do with your

gift?

2. If God can meet the needs of the multitude with very few resources, why do

we doubt his ability to meet our needs?

## Day 4: My Service to Others
*Read James* 3:13–18

"The wisdom that comes from heaven is first of all pure; then peace-loving, considerate, submissive, full of mercy and good fruit, impartial and sincere" (James 3:17). Gentleness is the greatest asset for those who want to minister to others. The great Phillips Brooks, all his life a bachelor, was a great pastor because he practiced a childlike gentleness.

On one occasion a young mother in his congregation had a baby—her first—but the baby was stillborn. The poor woman panicked and suffered a severe denial that would not let her face the facts. She clung to her dead baby and cowered in the corner of her room in a rocking chair. When anyone tried to take the baby away, she clung all the more fiercely. It finally became clear that the baby would have to be forcefully taken from her arms in a desperate and grasping scene. But then God intervened in the desperate situation.

Enter the gentle servant Phillips Brooks.

He walked to the woman's rocking chair, smiled kindly at her, and said, "What a beautiful child. Would you mind if I rocked her a while?"

He was so gentle and kind that the woman extended him the child, and to the surprise of all, Dr. Brooks took her seat in the rocker and tenderly rocked her baby.

An ugly crisis had been solved by a gentle spirit.

## Questions for Personal Reflection

1. How can gentleness help you avoid conflict?

2. Who are those people who personify gentleness in your life?

# Day 5: My Personal Worship
*Read Matthew 21:14–17*

On Palm Sunday, the children kept praising Jesus, but the priests couldn't stand it. Their gentle godliness was born out of their innocence, uncorrupted by any ambitious agenda. Children can indeed teach us how to worship.

One of my grandsons came to us from Bangkok when he was ten years old. His childhood had been spent as a Buddhist, and he was then thrown suddenly into a Christian family. He congenially attended our Christian church with us, and, upon much reflection, he said after church one day, "Mom, know why I like Jesus better than Buddha?"

"No," said his mother (my daughter). "Why?"

"Well," he replied, "Jesus could say to the storm, 'Peace be still,' and it got still. But Buddha, he doesn't do anything but just sit there."

In today's passage from Matthew, it seems Jesus was saying, "Some of the greatest insights are hidden from the scholars and revealed to the children."

But best of all is the gentle praise children offer God, as if every Sunday is Palm Sunday to them. They are always ready to crown him king. So true is their theology that when asked what the world's most impressive theological truth is, Karl Barth replied, "Jesus loves me, this I know—for the Bible tells me so."

## Questions for Personal Reflection

1. What is the simplest expression of your faith in God?

2. Do you ever make your relationship with God too complicated? In what ways?

# Day 6: Barnabas—Gentle Encouragement

*Read Acts 4:36–37; 11:19–24*

Barnabas was among the first of the wealthy patrons of the church. He sold a field and laid the money at the apostles' feet. He gave in a gentle and unobtrusive way that probably inspired the more self-seeking and less gentle Ananias and Sapphira to give in Acts 5. Barnabas's name meant "son of encouragement."

How exalted is this virtue, encouragement! We live in a world where criticism is customary and a good word of support is rare. But Barnabas was an encourager and distinguished himself by practicing the art of affirmation. Who knows what role he might have played in creating the New Testament as both John Mark and Paul's traveling companion. Encouragement is a gentle art, yet it often becomes a kind of silent survival for those who need it.

Acts 11:19–24 is an example of Barnabas's encouragement to the early church. The early church was multicultural. In this passage the thumbscrews of Jewish persecution had tightened upon the church following Stephen's martyrdom. As the pressure became intense, Jewish Christians left the Jerusalem area and scattered "as far as Phoenicia, Cyprus and Antioch" (v. 19). This meant that those who were scattered began to evangelize Gentiles where they had previously evangelized Jews. "The Lord's hand was with them, and a great number of people believed and turned to the Lord" (v. 21). With the stress of persecution so prevalent, it was a great day for encouragement.

Barnabas was there. "When he arrived and saw the evidence of the grace of God, he was glad and encouraged them all to remain true to the Lord with all their hearts" (v. 23). Barnabas used some good old-fashioned affirmation to strengthen those who had been saved.

But there was one other advantage. Gentleness itself is a soul-winner. This passage says Barnabas was "a good man, full of the Holy Spirit and faith, and a great number of people were brought to the Lord" (v. 24). Gentleness is the tool that encouragement uses to evangelize. Most people are not led to the Lord by carefully crafted, hard-core arguments, but by gentle listening. People who are affirmed and encouraged often rush into the arms of a Savior of whom they are not afraid. Barnabas encouraged such faith. Gentleness was his method.

Can we win the world to Christ? Yes, if we straighten our doubled fists into open hands; if we unclench our face and smile at those who need Jesus; if we don't try to *argue* souls into the kingdom of God but *listen* to them instead.

Encourage others and you will not be like Barnabas, but like Jesus. Compliment the unappreciated. Affirm the unnoticed. Affirmation is the quickest path to the heart of God.

## Questions for Personal Reflection

1. Who are those people who encourage you? In what ways are you encouraged by them?

2. Are there people for whom you are an encourager? If so, what do you do to encourage them?

# Day 7: Group Discussion

The following questions should take about forty-five minutes to answer and discuss. Each member should answer the first question, leaving the remaining questions open-ended. Everyone need not answer, but be sure all members participate.

1.   *How have you seen God approach you, or someone else, gently?*

2.   *How might our practice of faith change if we approached it as little children?*

3.  *What do you have that you could offer to God? What might God do with your offering?*

4.  *What does godly wisdom produce in our lives? How do we know when we see wisdom in action?*

5.  *How does it make you feel to know that you are God's child? What privileges come with that status?*

6.  *What are some ways we can become better encouragers to others who are serving God?*

## Week 5: Gentleness—The Healing Touch of God

*Memory Passage for the Week: Isaiah 11:9*

### Day 1: Gentleness—The Healing Touch of God

Jesus healed a woman who did nothing more than touch the hem of his garment. Mark 5:24–34.

### Day 2: The Purpose of God in My Life

God has been gentle with his people for generations. He is gentle, and we should follow suit. 1 Chronicles 16:8, 19–22.

### Day 3: My Relationship with Christ

God gently makes all things new and restores our relationship with Jesus and our world. John 20:21–22.

### Day 4: My Service to Others

Elijah was a tender healer of bereavement and lost hope. This is the sort of gentleness with which we are to serve each other. 1 Kings 17:17–24.

### Day 5: My Personal Worship

John told his tale of Jesus in such a gentle fashion that not even a child would be afraid to hear it. 1 John 1:1–4.

### Day 6: The Parable of the Weeds

Matthew 13:24–30 (TLB)

### Day 7: Group Discussion

## Day 1: Gentleness—The Healing Touch of God
*Read Mark 5:24–34*

Jesus healed a woman who did nothing more than touch the hem of his garment. Gentleness meets urgency in this desperate tale of hope and healing. Gentleness: the delicate feel of linen fabric on desperate, reaching fingertips. Gentleness: Christ felt the virtue leave his body, but he replied in gentleness too.

Behind this gentleness was the frantic need of a woman who had spent all her life seeing physicians. When her money was gone and there was no one else to turn to, when every doctor had failed to heal her, she sought a gentle healer. As I once wrote in a previous work of mine, these might have been her words:

> *I struggled just to touch*
> *Him, in my frail attack*
> *Against the crowd so much around.*
> *They shoved me back.*

> *In weakened fury there*
> *I tore the people wall.*
> *I clawed the frenzied air.*
> *The Savior seemed so tall.*

*Yet through that madding crowd,*
*I could not seem to probe*
*The human press. I'd vowed*
*My hand should touch his robe.*

*And then the instant came!*
*The wall gave way. The tide*
*Fell back. I breathed his name*
*In freedom at his side.*

*I fell with hands outstretched*
*And felt his tunic there.*
*The crowd moved by a wretch*
*Who breathed a strange new air.*[3]

## Questions for Personal Reflection

1. What is your most desperate cry to God?

2. How do you expect God to respond to your desperate plea?

# Day 2: The Purpose of God in My Life

*Read 1 Chronicles 16:8, 19–22*

David, in this psalm, rejoiced with Israel over the gentle leadership of God. God had, after all, found them in the wilderness and gently led them to Canaan. The Exodus might seem anything but gentle; nevertheless it *was* gentle. When Hosea pictured it, he wrote:

> *When Israel was a child, I loved him*
> > *and out of Egypt I called my son.*
> *But the more I called Israel,*
> *the further they went from me.*
> *It was I who taught Ephraim to walk,*
> *taking them by the arms;*
> *but they did not realize*
> *it was I who healed them.*
> *I led them with cords of human kindness,*
> > *with ties of love;*
> *I lifted the yoke from their neck,*
> > *and bent down to feed them.*
> —Hosea 11:1–4

This tender picture of a Father with a little boy is as gentle as this psalm of thanksgiving:

*Give thanks to the* LORD, *call on his name.*

*When they were but few in number,*

*few indeed, and strangers in it,*

*They wandered from nation to nation,*

*from one kingdom to another,*

*He allowed no man to oppress them;*

*for their sake he rebuked kings:*

*Do not touch my anointed ones;*

*do my prophets no harm.*

—1 Chronicles 16:8, 19–22

These gentle Scriptures are clear: God is gentle and we should follow suit.

## Questions for Personal Reflection

1. What is the one thing for which you are most thankful? How do you express

that thanksgiving to God?

2. What are some things for which you should be more thankful?

# Day 3: My Relationship with Christ

*Read John 20:21–22*

Long ago I happened to be in Brussels, Belgium, on Pentecost, the day when the world celebrates the coming of the Holy Spirit. The great Pentecostal passage was read from Acts, and for a moment I felt that awesome unity that makes people of all nationalities one. It happened in the book of Acts on the very day the Spirit first came.

Standing there in the Brussels church, I thought of how long ago Jesus breathed on his disciples and said to them, "Receive the Holy Spirit!" and they did. Suddenly, in that great cathedral, I realized:

> *Pentecost is not merely a day on the church calendar; it is fire and wind able to blow anytime. The elation is inebriating. It comes suddenly like the wind of which Jesus said, "The wind bloweth where it listeth, and thou hearest the sound thereof, but cannot tell whence it cometh or whither it goeth; so is everyone who is born of the Spirit (KJV)." And like the Jerusalem pilgrims in the book of Acts, our elation must make us appear as though we have "gotten drunk on God," and the joy binds the ages."[1]*

The gentle breath of God fills us with great power. But more than that it fills us with an even greater hunger to be breathed on again and again.

*Holy Spirit, breathe on me,*

*Until my heart is clean.*

*Let sunshine fill its inmost part*

*With not a cloud between.*

—"Holy Spirit, Breathe On Me"

Words by Edwin Hatch

## Questions for Personal Reflection

1. How does the Holy Spirit empower you?

2. What happens when you try to do something without the power of God's

Spirit?

# Day 4: My Service to Others
*Read 1 Kings 17:17–24*

"O LORD my God, let this boy's life return to him!" (1 Kings 17:21). With the prophet's gentle cry, God restored a dead boy to life. Christ's followers exist to make dead things live. We have no power to do this, but as we touch lifeless things, Christ who lives in us gives life through us, and then beyond us.

We touch dead worship, and if we are in touch with Christ, the living center, then the whole body of Christ comes alive.

We touch dead hope, and those who had given up hope can see that the church exists to make a needy world more alive.

We touch a child with affirmation, and that child—who may be dying for a compliment—is suddenly more alive.

We touch an old woman in a nursing home—a woman who has waited in vain for anyone to call—and suddenly Jesus is all around us, using our touch to make lifeless eyes sparkle and dull hearts beat again.

Gentleness is our calling. We are to go where people are afraid and leave them without fear. We are to go where there is no food, and feed. We are to go to the needy and clothe them. But above all, we are to do these things gently, not roaring about our own goodness or swaggering over our biblical knowledge. We are the gentle hands who touch with the hand of Jesus. We trust the touch of Christ, for it changed us. Now we must give it for the sake of all those yet unhealed.

## Questions for Personal Reflection

1. In what ways can we bring the "dead" back to life?

2. How has God calmed your fears? How can you help calm the fears of others?

# Day 5: My Personal Worship

*Read 1 John 1:1–4*

The sensate feeling in this passage is too real to be denied. John's books were written at a time when Gnosticism was rampant. One of the chief Gnostic heresies was Docetism (from the Greek *dokeo*, "to seem"). Docetists taught that Jesus wasn't really a man, but only seemed to be so; to them he was really a ghostly messiah who never really became flesh and blood.

John wanted to combat this notion. Notice the sensate ways he speaks of how the early church actually encountered the living Christ (1 John 1:1–4).

Christ, whom we heard (v. 3).

Christ, whom we saw with our eyes (v. 1).

Christ, whom we touched with our hands (v. 1).

Here is the Christ, whose gentle being is reported so honestly, yet powerfully enough to propel the church forward for thousands of years to come.

But notice the epigram to the apostle's testimony. This hearable, seeable, touchable Christ is real. His reality, gentle and certain, is vitality to the church victorious.

Sunday by Sunday as we come to worship, we may have confidence that the Bible is true: John and the witnesses certified it. May we be as gentle in our ministry of certainty as John was in reporting it.

## Questions for Personal Reflection

1. How would you defend the reality of Christ?

2. What is God doing in your life right now?

# Day 6: The Parable of the Weeds

## Matthew 13:24–30 (TLB)

The Kingdom of Heaven is like a farmer sowing good seed in his field; but one night as he slept, his enemy came and sowed thistles among the wheat. When the crop began to grow, the thistles grew too.

The farmer's men came and told him, "Sir, the field where you planted that choice seed is full of thistles!"

"An enemy has done it," he exclaimed.

"Shall we pull out the thistles?" they asked.

"No," he replied. "You'll hurt the wheat if you do. Let both grow together until the harvest, and I will tell the reapers to sort out the thistles and burn them, and put the wheat in the barn."

## Questions for Personal Reflection

1. Are you the wheat or the thistles? What is your ministry to the thistles in your

midst?

2. How can you apply the truth of this parable to your life?

# Day 7: Group Discussion

The following questions should take about forty-five minutes to answer and discuss. Each member should answer the first question, leaving the remaining questions open-ended. Everyone need not answer, but be sure all members participate.

1.  *What might change in your life if you received a fresh breath of the Holy Spirit?*

2.  *How can we apply the truth of the parable of the weeds to our lives?*

3.  *What causes us to celebrate God's work in our lives?*

4.  *What causes us not to have confidence in our prayers? Is it a problem with us or a problem with God? Explain your response.*

5.  *What do we know to be true about God? How do you know what is true?*

6.  *Who are the modern Gnostics and how should we respond to them?*

# Week 6: Jesus—The Model of Gentleness

*Memory Passage for the Week: Isaiah 40:29*

### Day 1: Jesus—The Model of Gentleness

Christ is gentle in his magnificent redemption of the planet. Isaiah 6:1–8.

### Day 2: The Purpose of God in My Life

Given the nature of this world's tyrants, how welcome a king is Jesus, with his fearless touch and warm smile. Isaiah 42:1–4.

### Day 3: My Relationship with Christ

We have an unbreakable relationship with Christ. Who has walked with Christ and not found the walking sweet? Isaiah 43:1–2.

### Day 4: My Service to Others

Jesus is a model for how the compassionate are called to serve the needy. We are Jesus' hands and feet. We are his servants. His ministry of comfort and hope has been laid upon us. Isaiah 49:8–13.

### Day 5: My Personal Worship

Come in adoration and thank God for the provisions of this life which he provides so graciously for us. This is our call to worship. Isaiah 55:1–2, 6–7.

### Day 6: Verses for Further Reflection

### Day 7: Group Discussion

# Day 1: Jesus—The Model of Gentleness
*Read Isaiah 6:1–8*

*Gentleness*, in the best New Testament sense of the word, could be defined as "power under control." It is the image of a great stallion under the rein of a small and light jockey. A great horse is controlled by the simplest tug on the rein. In the strictest sense of the word, gentleness does not imply inferiority. Yet who among us isn't plagued by feelings of inferiority from time to time?

Isaiah protested with his spiritual inferiority, thinking it would negate his noble call.

"Woe to me!" he cried. "I am ruined! For I am a man of unclean lips, and I live among a people of unclean lips, and my eyes have seen the King, the LORD Almighty" (Isaiah 6:5). God has a way of dealing with our sense of inferiority, helping us rise above our whipped feelings. In this image of cleansing, the prophet threw out his lame excuses:

"Then one of the seraphs flew to me with a live coal in his hand, which he had taken with tongs from the altar. With it he touched my mouth and said, 'See, this has touched your lips; your guilt is taken away and your sin atoned for'" (vv. 6–7). And with this searing image, Isaiah's inferiority was taken away and he was ready to serve. Thus, when God said, "Whom shall I send? And who will go for us?" ... Isaiah was ready to answer, "Here am I, send me" (v. 8).

Isaiah left the Old Testament's finest picture of what the Messiah would look like when he arrived. The Old Testament foreshadows the Messiah with two images. The first was the regal image of King David, who stood as the symbol of a kingly Messiah; this Warrior Messiah led a vast conquering army to establish his eternal reign of peace with authority, and allowed no evil to exist.

But the other role was illustrated in Isaiah's picture of a gentle, suffering-servant Messiah. This Messiah would take upon himself the pain of the world. He would bear the sins of the people. He would cleanse the world of pride, leaving nothing in evil's place but a gentle response to the love of God. Jesus perfectly fulfills this picture in his pure life and sacrificial death. He never sought a shred of fame or power for himself. Christ is gentle in his magnificent redemption of the planet.

## Questions for Personal Reflection

1. Do you typically associate gentleness with weakness or strength?

2. Why is gentleness not a sign of inferiority? How does God reveal this truth to us?

# Day 2: The Purpose of God in My Life
*Read Isaiah 42:1–4*

Isaiah in time would become one of Israel's greatest poets. His poet's heart always left him insecure, but his insecurity burst forth in a thousand poems that glorified God from the center of his gentle spirit. So Isaiah's gentleness praises God forever. Out of such gentleness he praised the suffering and Gentle Redeemer servant:

> *Here is my servant, whom I uphold,*
> > *my chosen one in whom I delight;*
> *I will put my Spirit on him*
> > *and he will bring justice to the nations.*
> *He will not shout or cry out,*
> > *or raise his voice in the streets.*
> *A bruised reed he will not break,*
> > *and a smoldering wick he will not snuff out.*
> *In faithfulness he will bring forth justice;*
> > *he will not falter or be discouraged*
> *till he establishes justice on earth.*
> > *In his law the islands will put their hope.*
> —Isaiah 42:1–4

In this wonderful poem there exists a call. The call is yours—a call to be like Jesus. If Jesus is our Lord and role model in the arena of gentleness, do we have any right to become self-involved, unkind servants?

"No servant is greater than his master, nor is a messenger greater than the one who sent him" (John 13:16). Surely if Jesus was so tender as to not even crush a bruised reed, we are called to be the same, even when other Christians take a position that seems odd or unreasonable to us. We must not engage in name calling, shouting, or abusive speech. The purpose of God in our lives is to make us appear like Jesus, to be gentle in all our dealings.

## Questions for Personal Reflection

1. Can you think of a time when you did not portray the gentleness of Jesus and found yourself having to ask forgiveness for those you may have verbally abused?

2. What part did humility play in your forgiveness plea?

# Day 3: My Relationship with Christ

*Read Isaiah 43:1–2*

Here, in the book of Isaiah, are the four great values that lie at the heart of our relationship with Christ. These four values symbolize an unbreakable bond. This is the thrilling part! We aren't perfect when we come to him, and best of all, we don't have to be perfect to continue in our relationship with Jesus. When we meet Christ, we are unclean, unworthy, undedicated, and disobedient. And he requires of us no moral reform to enter his love forever. It is wonderful!

"Just as I am" is the deal. We come to him warts, wrinkles, and all, and he envelopes us with such a cleansing that we never recover from the wonder of it. We do nothing to earn God's glorious favor, but we can find ourselves lost in the wonder of an unbreakable relationship with Christ. Here is his fourfold promise:

🦌 First, he created us. We were, as the psalmist said, "Fearfully and wonderfully made" (Psalm 139:14). But in coming to the Gentle Christ, we are remade in his likeness. It's a lot to live up to, but a glorious state of existence.

🦌 Second, he redeemed us. This is the "dirty" work of a God set out to launder the human race. We were scrubbed up in the blood of Christ. We can answer yes to the question, "Have you been to Jesus for the cleansing power? Are you washed in the blood of the Lamb?"

We've been to the cleansing place. We are forever one with him.

🦌 Third, he calls us by name. Do you keep a little book with the names of all your friends? Jesus does, and you're in the book.

🦌 And fourth, the trials of life cannot chip the granite of this relationship. We hold a faith that water cannot drown and fire cannot burn.

What a friend we have! What love we share with the lover of our souls.

## Questions for Personal Reflection

1. What four words, different than these used by Isaiah, would you use to characterize your relationship with Christ?

2. What is the best example of Christ's presence you have known in your most extreme time of need?

# Day 4: My Service to Others
*Read Isaiah 49:8–13*

The Jewish captives, after their long imprisonment in Babylon and Persia, were free to return at last. God essentially said to the captives, "Come out!" and to those in darkness, "Be free!" These former slaves were like starving sheep that only knew drought, feeding on grassless hilltops and burnt-off fields. But refreshment was on the way—lush grass for the hungry flock.

We should serve each other as purveyors of hope. "This too shall pass!" is a phrase that encourages those whose despair cannot find the light. Then when it arrives, hope comes like the sunrise after a night of storms. Despair is over-estimated. It will not last forever.

In the book of Revelation there is a picture given to the martyrs of what would follow their bloody ordeals in the arena. Dying in blood for the sport of emperors was too great a horror without this divine picture:

> *Then one of the elders asked me, "These in white robes—who*
> *are they, and where did they come from?"*
> *I answered, "Sir, you know."*
> *And he said, "These are they who have*
> *come out of the great tribulation;*
> *they have washed their robes and*
> *made them white in the blood of the Lamb.*

*Therefore, they are before the throne of God*

*and serve him day and night in his temple....*

*Never again will they hunger;*

*never again will they thirst.*

*The sun will not beat upon them,*

*nor any scorching heat.*

*For the Lamb at the center of the*

*throne will be their shepherd;*

*he will lead them to springs of living water.*

*and God will wipe away every tear from their eyes."*

—Revelation 7:13–17

Isaiah in the Old Testament and John in the New Testament explained what service to others really is: we are the ministers of hope in an age of disconsolation. We are to stop the tears of the broken, and cry out to all, "Come out! Be free! Christ is on his throne!"

## Questions for Personal Reflection

1. Think about the fiercest night you have ever spent in tears, and answer this question: Who or what brought you ultimate consolation?

2. What part of your ministry to others is derived directly from your willingness simply to be present in the midst of someone else's need?

# Day 5: My Personal Worship

*Read Isaiah 55:1–2, 6–7*

Some of the greatest praise takes place right after we have received a great gift from God.

In Isaiah we hear the message of abundance to those who are poor and cannot afford the sumptuous fare the poem offers. Come without money; God provides. Come thirsty and drink! Come hungry and eat! Come empty and be filled!

Many people refer to God's provision as providence. There is a city in New England by that name—Providence. When New England was first settled, there was great suffering and hardship. More than half the passengers on the Mayflower, for instance, died on the passage to Plymouth Rock. These pilgrims endured harsh first winters on the bleak North American continent plagued with sickness and death.

But this was the birth of the word *providence*. Did God provide? He did ... in time. They saw that God held the same hope for them that Isaiah's exiles found when he asked them to come and eat and drink without cost.

In short, they worshiped. So do we!

Like the Israelites, we discover that water can gush from rocks. Manna can be born upon the ground. Seas can split. Walls can tumble down. And what do we do after each of these provident acts of God? We worship! We receive and then we cannot help ourselves. God must be praised.

## Questions for Personal Reflection

1. What are the three top events in your walk with Christ, where you received such an obvious answer to your prayers that you had no option except to praise?

2. How many times in a single lifetime do you think we really worship, as though our lives truly depend on God's supplying our need?

# Day 6: Verses for Further Reflection

**Matthew 5:5:** Blessed are the meek, for they will inherit the earth.

**Matthew 11:29:** Take my yoke upon you and learn from me, for I am gentle and humble in heart, and you will find rest for your souls.

**Matthew 18:3–4:** I tell you the truth, unless you change and become like little children, you will never enter the kingdom of heaven. Therefore, whoever humbles himself like this child is the greatest in the kingdom of heaven.

**Matthew 21:5:** Say to the Daughter of Zion, "See, your king comes to you, gentle and riding on a donkey, on a colt, the foal of a donkey."

**2 Corinthians 10:1:** By the meekness and gentleness of Christ, I appeal to you—I, Paul, who am "timid" when face to face with you, but "bold" when away!

**Ephesians 4:2:** Be completely humble and gentle; be patient, bearing with one another in love.

**Philippians 4:5:** Let your gentleness be evident to all. The Lord is near.

**1 Timothy 6:11:** But you, man of God, flee from all this, and pursue righteousness, godliness, faith, love, endurance and gentleness.

# PHILEMON 1:1, 8–21

*Paul encouraged his friend to be gentle and loving in his reception of runaway slave Onesimus. Gentleness is a virtue to celebrate. It goes beyond the letter of the law to exalt mercy.*

Paul, a prisoner of Christ Jesus, and Timothy our brother, to Philemon our dear friend and fellow worker.... Therefore, although in Christ I could be bold and order you to do what you ought to do, yet I appeal to you on the basis of love. I then, as Paul—an old man and now also a prisoner of Christ Jesus—I appeal to you for my son Onesimus, who became my son while I was in chains. Formerly he was useless to you, but now he has become useful both to you and to me.

I am sending him—who is my very heart—back to you. I would have liked to keep him with me so that he could take your place in helping me while I am in chains for the gospel. But I did not want to do anything without your consent, so that any favor you do will be spontaneous and not forced. Perhaps the reason he was separated from you for a little while was that you might have him back for good—no longer as a slave, but better than a slave, as a dear brother. He is very dear to me but even dearer to you, both as a man and as a brother in the Lord.

So if you consider me a partner, welcome him as you would welcome me. If he has done you any wrong or owes you anything, charge it to me. I, Paul, am writing this with my own hand. I will pay it back—not to mention that you owe me your very self. I do wish, brother, that I may have some benefit from you in the Lord; refresh my heart in Christ. Confident of your obedience, I write to you, knowing that you will do even more than I ask.

## Questions for Personal Reflection

1. How can you develop an intimate relationship with God?

2. How do you know when your relationship with God is weak?

# Day 7: Group Discussion

The following questions should take about forty-five minutes to answer and discuss. Each member should answer the first question, leaving the remaining questions open-ended. Everyone need not answer, but be sure all members participate.

1.  *When people encounter us, they either see Jesus or something else. What are those other things they see, and how can we keep from misrepresenting God to the world?*

2.  *For what purpose do you feel God has called you?*

3. *Who are the people who need our consoling?*

4. *Where can we go to encounter the brokenhearted?*

5. How can we become more aware of God's providence in our lives? What do we mistakenly call events that are consistent with his providence?

6. What are some things we can do to guard our spiritual lives against decay? What can we do to strengthen our spiritual lives?

## ENDNOTES

1. *Calvin Miller, Poem quoted from* The Owner's Manual for the Unfinished Soul *(Wheaton, IL: Harold Shaw Publishers, 1997),* 107.

2. *Author Unknown,* The Coventry Carol, *(New York, NY: Simon & Schuster, 1996),* 158–59.

3. *Calvin Miller, Poem quoted from* An Owner's Manual for the Unfinished Soul *(Wheaton, IL: Harold Shaw Publishers, 1997),* 96.

4. *Calvin Miller, Poem quoted from* An Owner's Manual for the Unfinished Soul *(Wheaton, IL: Harold Shaw Publishers, 1997),* 93–94.

# PRAYER JOURNAL

*Use the following pages to record both prayer requests and answers.*

# PRAYER JOURNAL